Pondering Stars
on the Pond

Kim, Junghwa Splendor (1970)
Pondering Stars on the Pond [paperback]

1st ed. – New York: Five Points Publishing, 2025: 122 p.: 8 x 5 inches.

ISBN: 979-8-9991142-0-4.

Pondering Stars on the Pond
© Junghwa Splendor Kim
© Five Points Publishing
250 East 34th Street, New York, NY 10016
USA

Cover design: Camila Jara
Editor: Felipe Hugueño

First edition: May, 2025.
First reprint: October, 2025.

Printed or digital reproduction of this work is expressly prohibited without the consent of its author or publisher.

Pondering Stars on the Pond

Junghwa Splendor Kim

SHIRT TAILS

poetry collection

Table of Contents

Preface. Diaspora and Creation 11

I. Heart and Muse 17

   Love in a *Cursive Font* 19
   In the Shadow of Your Bloom 20
   Your Voice 21
   Bookmark's Vigil 22
   In Search of the Sphere 24
   Emotional Fusion 25
   Notes on a Kiss 27
   Entitled 28
   Night Creator 29
   A Season Not to Fall 30
   The Interpreter's Stanza 31
   The Kernel and the Flesh 32
   My Ideal Robot Companion 34
   A Virgin at the Altar 36
   Autumn Jazz: Special Edition 38
   Subway Fantasy 39
   The Fabric of Us 41
   Song of Peace 43

Under This Shared Sky 44
Where Two Paths Converge 45
Awakening to the Nectar of Time 46
Raison d'être 48
Valentino's Heavenly Walks 50
A Fair Equation 52
Love of Three Millennia 54
Island Nostalgia 56
Sweet Teen, Evergreen 57
How to Miss Me: A Manual 58

II. Heartache and Melancholy 59

Attitude Toward Goodbye 61
Unseen in Your Gaze 63
The Boomerang of Silence 64
An Icy Land of Silence 65
Portrait of a City Dweller 66
Mirage 69
Across the Date Line 70
Between the Waves 71
Sipping on Solitude 73
Erasing Your Name 74
Protocol for Your Return 76
May I Ask you A Favor? 77

Teardrops in the Crowd 78
Fade Out..79
A Heart in Grayscale..80
Winy Silence Along the Vines 82
Farewell, in the Gale..83
A Masochist's Love Song....................................84

III. Nature and Gaze 85

Heartbeat of Poetry..87
The Language of Omega 88
Questions of Alchemy of Six Elements 89
Black Pearl...91
Jade 92
Sunflower's Identity 93
An Interview with a Poet 94
Hydrotherapy..95
Ode to Vanity..96
A Story Behind the Altar of Poetry..................97
A Prehistoric Song from the Cave 98
The Hermit's Thesis...99
Into the Spring Light..100
Library Philosopher..101
The Tapestry of Sunshine and Shade 102
Invisible Yet Visible...104

From the Golden Hill 106
Zafira, the Minimalist................................. 107
To My Supreme Sphere 108
Meditation on Peeing 109
Dandelion's Blaze.. 110
Along the Veins of Nature............................ 112
A Butterfly in Blue 113
The Captain's Song 115

Epilogue 117
Acknowledgements.. 119

Preface
Diaspora and Creation

Brother Anthony of Taizé
Emeritus Professor of English Literature at Sogang University in South Korea; Translator of Korean Literature into English

In recent years, there has been much talk about the special characteristics of the writing of the Korean Diaspora. There has, of course, for long been a Korean Diaspora. Before 1900, some young Koreans were already studying in the United States and not all returned home. Early in the 1900s, thousands of young Korean men went to work in the plantations of Hawaii with no thought of returning home either. Instead, after more than ten years of solitude, they were joined by "picture brides," mostly poor young Korean girls from rural villages who dreamed of finding wealth and education. They were often disappointed. During the Japanese colonial period, many were forced to go to other parts of the Japanese empire to work, culminating in the tragic histories of so many women, while more fortunate young Koreans went to study modernity in Japan or China, if not in North America. A great Diaspora followed in the decades after the Korean War as well, when many families, even those with higher education, felt that they could earn more and live more rewarding lives by opening small stores in California or New York.

Among those thus uprooted, either voluntarily or forcibly, there were some who felt summoned to write, either directly about or in emotional response to their uprooting. The first-generation writers had to confront the inner tensions of life away from their childhood setting and culture, living in a world whose language they had not had the time to master fully. Inwardly, they could not avoid wondering what was their essential identity, divorced as they were from the evolutions of contemporary Korean history. No matter how fluent their new language skills were, that was not their mother tongue, not the language of their earliest memories.

They had to choose whether to write in the Korean language they brought with them and which they could use at home, if they lived as a family, or whether to express themselves in the language of the place they now inhabited. If they wrote in Korean, only Koreans could read what they wrote, in the Diaspora or back at home. For many, that was not a problem. Yet for others, the call was to communicate with the wider society of their new homeland, using their new language, one that might reach even other countries besides the one they lived in, becoming universal.

At the same time, if they were writing poetry, there was a great difference between the poems they had read or heard in Korea and those they might read in their new country, especially if they studied literature at a higher level. The Western classics are very unlike anything that exists in Korea. The USA has always been the main center for the Korean Diaspora and the resulting poets and writers have long been known and admired in Korea, whether using English or Korean. Junghwa Splendor Kim is in a very different situation. Chile is her second home; Latin-American literature is her main reference. Spanish, French, English and Korean are all languages she uses in writing. She writes, then, in a very different complex of influences, less familiar in Korea, more diverse and challenging.

For her as for many first-generation Diaspora poets, poetic voice is an enormous challenge. No matter which language she uses, the foreignness is there. She may refer obliquely to famous Korean poems, even quote from them, but her readers who are not Korean will make nothing of her references. After many years of living in another tongue and culture, one's native tongue loses its immediate references, and one's cultural references become more or less fossilized. Therefore, the most important question is how to create poetry beyond the conventions of any particular national poetic tradition.

As a speaker of four languages, with Korean as her mother tongue, the poetic world of Junghwa Splendor Kim is enriched by the diversity and dynamics of the other languages she speaks, with their influences constantly weaving together. The poetry she writes in English will remain poetry if transformed by her into Spanish, French or Korean. For her, the act of translation and the act of creation remain one, since she is translating her own words to produce her own words. That is not true when a translator translates another's poetry.

Junghwa Splendor Kim is the Korean Diaspora incarnate, full of loss and gain, pain and triumph, transcending every limitation of nationality and language to celebrate the world seen by a poet in eternal exile.

I
Heart and Muse

Love in a *Cursive Font*

When love flourishes,
The couple sits beside the well.
Though no water is drawn, it overflows,
And even without a deep drink,
Love quenches the heart's thirst.

Love's words flow like cursive script,
Even with eyes closed, they rise in a whirl,
And when the eyes open, they settle into a dream.
The sentence of love is a paradox:
What is beyond love is love itself.

A poet once whispered,
"I passed by briefly, unnoticed by you."
Love is like writing on a blade of grass,
Erasing, then rewriting, over and over
Until, through tears that cannot be suppressed.
The scent of overlapping grassy tendrils
Flows along the veins of the leaves.
Tangled together in a cursive font.

In the Shadow of Your Bloom

From the depths of my heart, a plant stirs to bloom,
An orchid of unquenchable desire, reaching for you.
It grows untamed, its roots run wild,
Fed by the ceaseless awe of your unravelling tone.
You extend beyond the measure of my being.

Your roots break free, weaving through my breath,
Transforming me—
I become a trunk, steadfast and strong,
I become the leaves, trembling in your song,
Until my body dissolves, wholly consumed,
Becoming the roots that anchor you.

Your Voice

Your voice is poetry,
A melody etched in lonely waves,
Soft as a noble valley's fold,
Rich with the scent of a freshly uncorked wine.
It is a symphony of disciplines intertwined—
Philosophy's questions, music's cadence,
Literature's whispers, linguistics' dynamics,
Chemistry's spark, psychology's depth.
Your voice carries fine art's grace,
Biology's pulse, ecology's breath,
Aesthetic wonder, theology's hymn,
The myths we dream, the tech we shape.

And within it all, a subtle melancholy—
The choreographed sway of belief and desire,
The inevitable touch of erotic fire.

Bookmark's Vigil

She devotes the full length of her body
To the purpose entrusted to her.
When you, adrift in the labyrinth of your heart,
Seek a place to pause,
She offers a haven upon the page.
In the quiet, disguised as coincidence,
Surely a prophetic line lies concealed.
You'll stumble upon a phrase like a compass,
And perhaps, collapsing in that very spot,
It becomes the kindling for your rise.

Until summoned again by her master's need,
She lingers unmoving for days,
Sometimes for years, or eternity itself.
A bridge between two worlds of thought,
She recites the lines she spans
Like a mantra, ceaselessly,
Imprinting her essence upon the words,
Whispering under the stars,
Yearning for your return.

Each night, amid the forest of language,

In the thickets of stories,

She stands naked,

Fulfilling her vertical mission as assigned,

Dreaming of the moment

Your horizontal hand will turn the page,

Waiting for that psychedelic, soulful, sweet touch.

In Search of the Sphere

The morning awakens with raindrops' babble,
Words stirring, unbound, seeking to travel.
Oh, Freedom! Unfurl the vastness of space,
Unleash its magnitude, its infinite grace.

Your voice, a dream, a coral reef's whisper,
I yearn to dissolve, to be one with it all—
Poured into your glass, coursing your veins,
Lost in the rhythm where breath entertains.

My thirst is drawn to those crimson streams,
Each droplet a key to violet dreams.
Beloved, let me be sealed in your flood,
Forever enshrined in the depths of your blood.

Emotional Fusion

Autumn flowers infused with the dreamy sunbeam,
A lively French jazz tune beside a pensive poem,
A woman's voice resembles that of a white wine poured slow,
A man's hand caresses her silky hair,

The curtain rises—a long-awaited rite,
Tremulous union on the edge of the night.
The man shivers before he dares to touch,
Her eyes glisten, dimmed by tears' soft clutch.

A heart meets a heart.
A soul folds into another soul.
Solitude caresses solitude.
A sigh of pleasure echoes like sobbing.

Desire aches for an everlasting truce,
While love's chemistry stirs and deludes—
Desire, frenzy, addiction, chaos,
All mistaken for love's pure seed.

Love is a thirst.
Love is a surge.
Love is a fairytale, a hunger,
A yearning for forever.

As the fan's gentle gust sways in this sphere,
Two lives merge into one, Nirvana clear,
Emotionally bound, eternally whole,
Where love is the union of body and soul.

Notes on a Kiss

What lingers unspoken, a weight on your heart,
Unshaped, unformed, defying all art—
What logic can't untangle, chaos can't mend,
A secret kept close, a truth without an end.

What twists through centuries, cloaked in mist,
Unborn as words, unsung as a myth,
No melody shapes it, no artist's hand,
No history claims it, no voice can command.

What haunts the deep dreams of mermaids,
What poets can't fathom, mathematicians can't keep,
What philosophers ponder, astrologers miss—
All these particles dissolve in a soulful kiss.

Entitled

Apricot blooms along the spring sun,
Stars find solace in the well,
Honey melds with ginger,
The microphone calls to the singer,
Water quenches the thirsty tongue,
Fallen leaves inspire the poet,
Tears soften weary eyes,
Moisturizer soothes dry skin,
Cream heals the weary toes,
And longing reaches for love's nest—
Each deserves to be cherished.

Having pondered these timeless connections
For what feels like eternity,
I know now,
I, too,
Am worthy of being truly loved by you.

Night Creator

A quiet truth sways to and fro,
Lost within the depths of your abyss.
Tonight, as before,
You stand beneath the shadowed shelter
Of coconut trees shrouded in night,

This newborn moment brushes softly
Against the sphere that is your soul.
The horizon hums with a magic tune,
A melody spun from nostalgia's lace.
A blossom of peace whispers to your ego,
And your essence merges with a greater truth.

Tonight, once more,
The ocean wind stirs,
Breathing the film of days long past.
A mirage dances on the shore,
Unfurling, stretching,
Toward the waiting galaxy.

You, the Night Creator.

A Season Not to Fall

This autumn, I hear the twilight weep,
Tears shed by the leaves as they fall from their keep,
Fearing the loss of the tree's cradle,
Drifting alone in the vast, cold space.

I am the leaf, and you are the tree,
Rooted deep, steady, holding me.
This autumn, I long to dissolve in your core,
To lose myself, to be yours once more.

But if to meld is too much to ask,
Grant me an adhesive, a bond to grasp—
A thread to hold through during autumn's sigh,
Until winter comes, and we say goodbye.

The Interpreter's Stanza

The road of the interpreter—
A divine magic that transforms
A spectrum of rays into a clearer light,
Stronger, brighter, reaching beyond sight.

An interpreter is a poet
Who decodes the language of thought,
A musician who understands
The note of silence, deeply sought.

An interpreter is an artist
Who feels the color of subtle nuance,
A dancer who knows
The gesture of the valuable art of balance

An interpreter is a prophet
Who grasps the chaos of foresight.

I am an interpreter.
My deepest wish is with this aligned—
To better decode the language of your mind.

The Kernel and the Flesh

* Inspired by the discovery that the green color of the avocado flesh is preserved when it remains united with its pit (kernel).

You are my kernel; I am your flesh.
As long as you stayed deep inside me,
I would remain untouched, a fresh, green bloom.

But one day, I was sliced into a salad,
Mashed into the dish,
And you wept for me,
Feeling the distress of being unable to lift me up.

Two bodies, yearning to be one,
Two hearts, hoping to unite.
We've fluttered together in time,
Lived together in harmony,
And when the end comes,
We will die together,
In the same nest, forever bound.

I nurse your scratch with tenderness,
For in this moment,
One day feels like eternity.

My Ideal Robot Companion

Give me a robot endowed with:
The unyielding strength to lift even a drunken elephant,
The expertise to steer a truck brimming with coal
Through the icy Andes in winter;
The serious presence of footsteps,
Like a thousand pounds,
When standing before someone cherished;
The gentle warmth to sit quietly
beside a tearful girl at a gloomy port,
Offering silent comfort;
Eyes that glimmer like a solitary star
Piercing the pitch black skies;
The fearless resolve
To fend off hornets from a summer book;
The resonant tones of a dawn mass,
Carrying the purity of a tranquil chant;
And the profound essence
That ties all these qualities together.
A being that navigates each day with flawless precision,
Unacquainted with the very notion of "fatigue."

An adventurer who roams freely,
Bridging the gaps between time and space.

A masterful writer, crafting ten pages
Of tender, poetic letters daily,
In Arial, size 10, with 1.5 line spacing.

An amazing multitasker, never failing in its mission,
Pledging unwavering loyalty each day,
Confidently reporting its readiness without exception.
A presence that fills the world with joy,
Promising boundless love for eternity.
This is the robot companion I envision.

The HOPE 21 ULTRA-PREMIUM, the latest model.
Where on earth is it available?

A Virgin at the Altar

The night the moonlight enchants me,
I will stretch upon the divine altar,
Shrouded in cloth of purest white,
Soft, radiant, and bright.

The night I drink deeply from dewdrops,
Tears will fall in secret streams,
The clearest, glossiest tears,
Hidden from the priest's gaze.

The night my body becomes an offering,
The sun will turn into the moon,
The moon to fire,
Fire to water,
Water to tree,
Tree to iron,
Iron to soil.

Sky and earth will exhale in wild rhythm,
Until linear time arches into a circle,
The circle spins into a sphere,
And the sphere is reborn as moonlight again.

When the universe's moments condense,
They will scatter as red dewdrops
On the altar's white cloth.
I, your virgin,
Lie waiting through the endless night,
Dreaming of silvery lavas surging forth,
Listening for the echo
From the deepest heart of the cosmos.

Tonight,
The universe dreams in red and white.

Autumn Jazz: Special Edition

Set me free, my Autumn, my Adam,
With your tranquil warmth, your noble tints,
Your sweeping vistas, your wisdom in falling,
Your artistry of change, your regal melancholy,
Your tender echoes of love, your quiet tears.

All that you are—your shapes and shadows—
Fuse with my soul, take root in my flesh.

Oh, my Adam, my Autumn,
Kiss me endlessly,
Until winter's breath arrives.

Subway Fantasy

Did you see me?
Have I wandered through your wild, untamed thoughts?
Do you sense my proximity, so close, yet so fleeting?
Or is it an illusion—a trick of time and space?

Are you truly there?
Am I truly here?
Do I still breathe in this trembling in-between?

Will your "here" and my "here"
Collide somewhere, someday?
Will our four arms intertwine,
Lost in the warmth of fusion?

Oh, we must part for now,
But will you stand at the same gate tomorrow?
Do you feel this frozen earth beneath me,
The burning roots twisting within?

Will you read these words someday,

Under the same rain-soaked skies?
I carry this big blue umbrella,
Hoping it catches your eye—
Hoping it stirs a memory of romance.
Darling, I see you each morning,
When my weary eyes crave dreams anew.
You turn up, and you turn me on,
Shaping my mornings into bluish dawns.

So I'll wait for you, tomorrow and beyond,
In this mystic rainy *rendezvous*,
Mon amour.

The Fabric of Us

You are my Prelude and Postlude,
The Thirst that drives me, the Wisdom that brightens me,
My Evolution's spark, my Revolution's fire,
The voice of my Pronunciation, the order in my Grammar,
My Emotion's depth, my Logic's clarity,
The Noun I name, the Verb I act on.

You are my Literature's senses, my Science's pulses,
The Dream that cuddles me, the Awakening that frees me,
My Womb of creation, my Tomb of meditation,
The Hypnosis that binds me, the Insomnia that wakes me.

You are my Fingerprint's pattern, my Footprint's trail,
My Inspiration's flame, my Aspiration's claim,
The Mast that lifts me, the Anchor that grounds me,

My Ego's strength, my Alter ego's whisper,
The Decision I choose, the Hesitation I ponder,
The Text I write, the Context I find,
My Vanity's gleam, my Insanity's stream.

Song of Peace

Once, there was peace in Eden,
No need for rules beneath the sky,
No pacts to mend, no tears to cry,
Only harmony, serenity, and coziness.

In the name of peace,
Nature's law flowed softly as spring's warm breeze,
Whispering by rivers where your smile
Shines a green splendor.

In the name of repose,
Music, poetry, and art became one,
Balancing spirits under the sun,
A tranquil hymn, a battle undone.

Once, there was peace in Eden.
And now, here, it blooms anew—
As long as the light in your eyes glows,
For love, for the world.

Under This Shared Sky

Existing side by side through the ages,
Beneath the same vast sky.
I breathe the air that belongs to us both,
With every breath, your smile appears before my eyes.

With every step, your whisper fills the air,
We share dreams born from solitude,
Beneath the same sky, we walk in silence,
Trusting in each other, forevermore.

Two hearts, one soul,
Under the same sun's warmth,
Blessed by the same moonlight,
Tempted by the same stars.

We share each breath we take,
We exist within the same shadow.
Together, forever,
Under this shared sky.

Where Two Paths Converge

Softness and wildness,
Shyness and courage,
The breath between us, horizontal and sentimental,
The energy within us, rising and boundless.

Let the rain fall upon the jungle,
Let the storm rage across the prairie.

Come closer, and dim the light,
Listen to the rhythm of our chemistry,
The tears have long passed,
Only the echo of peace remains,
Resonating in the deepest valley,
Floating gently outside the *fjord*.

Come, my soul,
Let us dive into the infinite,
The ocean of discovery,
The ocean of empathy,
The ocean of sweet surrender.

Awakening to the Nectar of Time

A touch of empathy, a hue of serendipity, a scent of philosophy, a whisper of fantasy,
A secret of luxury, a sense of mystery, a zenith of clarity, a whirl of chemistry,

All this stirs at once from your sacred form.
Man, you've waited years—perhaps a decade
Just to please me: solely, densely, peacefully, hopefully.
To unravel the formula of oneness between us.

Your body, the essence of truth,
The eternal youth's lust forever.
Crushed, mashed, and squeezed,
Only to be reborn as this splendor.

You are the true spirit of sacrifice,
Patience, and mercy.
How did you appear in my life so late?
With such bravery and bashfulness…
Oh, Mr. Wine, Mr. Post-Grape, Mr. Nirvana,

At last, your crystalline form caresses the depths of my soul,
Only to drain the desolation,
Encrusted with the solitude of a long breath.

Raison d'être

Under the blazing sun,
The soul of a grape absorbs the light,
Building strength within its being,
Like the pure essence of the fruit itself.
Then, it turns away from the solar dazzle,
And enters the darkness of the oak barrel,
Where, in stillness and contemplation,
Time gently ferments.

The oak barrel eventually gives way,
Splitting open,
Revealing the grape's profound rebirth,
For the sake of someone's love, someone's solace,
Someone's celebration, someone's vanity,
Someone's oblivion, someone's revolution—
The intense scent of yeast fills the air in its purple core.

A heart, heavy with anguish, plays the harp,
Trying to quiet the raging desire,
Sewing up the wounds with delicate fabric,
Struggling to break free from obsession,

To cleanse the stubborn, unyielding ties of this life.
¡Salud!

Valentino's Heavenly Walks

* In memory of Valentino, the beloved companion doggie of my friend, René Sinclair

In Heaven,
sunbeams carry a rainbow's scent,
the evening breeze cradles the quietest part of my soul.
Leaves wear their evergreen smiles.

Before my Heavenly breakfast,
I stroll with my Valentina,
past the Houses of Fantasy,
crafted by the Peace Creator,
built upon Pillars of Trust,
painted in hues of Generosity and Forgiveness,
adorned with the Peace of Mind,
all founded in Love.

In the afternoon, we swim through the honey-flavored rivers.

fruitful kisses and floral touches nourish our hearts.
This is Heaven, my love—
so please, don't weep like that.

A Fair Equation

Woman: Can we talk for a while?
Man: Is it truly important?
Woman: Importance is a practical word—
For someone like me, romance reigns.
Man: Is it urgent, then?
Woman: Conversation is not urgency.
It is sweetness I crave from you.
Man: Is sweetness indispensable?
Woman: Indeed, it is.
Will you offer it to me?
Man: How shall I be sweet to you?
Woman: Gaze infinitely into my soul,
Let eternity stretch—and one day more.
Man: I don't understand. Infinity, eternity—
Different measures of endlessness.
Why one day beyond eternity?
Woman: In case you forget love's language,
To restore lost time, to relearn its art.
Man: When does a man forget to love?
Woman: When sweetness fades.
Age plays no role.

Man: Then how can I be sweet?
Woman: Stroke my hair softly,
Whisper "I love you" into my waiting ear.
Man: What is love, truly?
Woman: It is romance and passion
Man: Then let me weigh your romantic and passionate body.
Woman: And my soul, as well.
(The room dims; the light fades.)

Love of Three Millennia

An oasis that endures for over three thousand years,
An ancient shrine where the tears and scars of a forgotten couple rest.
Their love, unfulfilled in this world, lingers in the air.
Love leaves behind its clues,
For those who understand its meaning,
Tears fall—some weep, some hide,
Before the sacred shrine.

Love, from long ago,
A blood-soaked oasis at the heart of time,
A power that reincarnates, a sign of immortality,
Through the ceaseless cycle of renewal.

Love forms Nirvana in the desert,
A beauty born from desperation,
A sorrow wrapped in grandeur.
Ah, love,
The name of aching beauty,
The name of sorrowful magnificence.

May it remain,
The never-ending current of passion.

Island Nostalgia

Tonight, beneath the island moon and my solitary sunset,
A poem stirs within me.
I breathe in the scent of *déjà-vu* from an unseen land.
In this forsaken space and time,
I long for the woodsy musk of your essence.

Tonight, I am a winter steppe wolf,
A nomad without a camel, without a fire,
Yearning to see my soul reflected in your eyes,
Yearning to feel my heartbeat echo in yours.

Tonight, I behold a frozen moon,
And under its cold gaze,
A poem begins to emerge in the dim moonlight,
Melting me, stanza by stanza.

Sweet Teen, Evergreen

If I held you close, would nectar drip from your being?
Is your essence a hive of golden sweetness?
I fear, as folktales whisper, that such sweetness might consume you.

I sustain myself on the honey of your body and soul.
In another life, I would be an evergreen sentinel,
A tree standing guard, offering solace and reflection,
Only to ease the tender strain of your sublime spirit,
Only to cradle your rest beneath my soothing, cooling shade.

How to Miss Me: A Manual

You should miss me like this:
My lips whispering "Splendorous!"
My third eye tracing the wild thoughts in your mind,
My breath, like jazz—unpredictable, irreconcilable,
My oriental wisdom, guiding your lost soul,
My humor sharp, like a rainbow's tasteful wind,
My poetic logic, my chaotic reason, my primal poetry,
My cosmopolitan vision,
My knowledge that stirs awe,
My heart, vast as the ocean,
My abyss, deep with sentiment,
My gaze, meditative (whether truth or illusion),
My touch, tender and untamed.

So... you should miss me this way when I am gone.
Even while I am still nearby,
Even when I return.
Learn the manual by heart over and over.

II
Heartache and Melancholy

Attitude Toward Goodbye

If you ever choose to leave me,
I won't scatter azalea petals
along the path you tread.
Whether it's fatigue or something deeper,
if you must go,
I promise I won't wish for you to stumble
within ten miles of your journey.
If departure calls,
I won't become the sunset
painting the sky behind you.

Even if the petals are crushed,
their shape lost in the dust,
or the sunset fades into gray,
will the one that leaves ever glance back?
Will the one who has gone ever return?
Before the word "goodbye" is spoken,
its meaning has already flowed
through your veins like ink,
a permanent tattoo etched into your soul.
Even if I gather those weary tales
stained with sorrowful blood

and stitch them into a quilt,
will beauty ever be sewn
without bearing scars?

Go, just go.
Burn your body to nothingness.
Slash your heart into naught.
But when you leave,
choose wisely the storm you walk into,
the night when a bitter, jagged rainbow
emerges from the tempest.

I am not here to see you off,
So, take care.

Unseen in Your Gaze

In your eyes, I am absent.
In your eyes, there lingers a memory—
An incomprehensible tale,
A shadow that cannot be understood.

In your eyes, there is no lightness,
Only the taste of bitterness,
A reflection of time that remains unsolved.

In your eyes,
My empty heart mirrors back,
Forming a shape too vast to name.
In your eyes,
Not even you exist.

The Boomerang of Silence

Your silence is many sleepless nights,
It is a tree that bears no fruit,
It is a solitary chair,
It is a cold, distant gaze,
It is the weight of oblivion,
It is a sickness with no cure.
It is somber clouds,
Your silence is a fevered whirlwind.

So, I send you the boomerang of my own silence,
Infused with a sensual scent,
As my finest revenge.

An Icy Land of Silence

Your silence is the confusion of forgotten tongues,
A true Tower of Babel in its depth.
Your silence is the endless ellipsis,
A mute still life frozen in time.
Your silence is wine, empty of remembrance,
An icy land with no penguins in sight,
An arrow lodged deep in my torment,
The source of my bitter poetic fire.

Portrait of a City Dweller

His mind tangled in awkward grammar,
Muddled with misspelled words,
Sentences waiting for correction,
His life out of rhythm,
Like shoes too large or too small.
He wished for one more hole in his belt,
But the wish remained futile.
It felt as though the wind slipped in through one shoulder.
The tools to survive packed in his bag,
Yet the weight he carried
Was heavier than any burden.
Each step he took was strenuous—
His shoulders always leaning to one side.
Like a seamstress stitching all night,
Yet still unable to make even slippers,
A hollow emptiness clung to him.
He felt like an abandoned train at a forgotten station,
Alone in the snow,
An isolated island.
He longed to go somewhere,

But reality's fence kept him bound.
Perhaps someone beautiful would come,
To free him from this cage,
But like scattered autumn leaves,
He held no firm hope.
He lacked confidence in his speech,
Even without knowledge of grammar,
Syntax, or semantics,
He wished for someone who could understand him
Just by looking into his eyes.
But then he shook his head—
Who would come?
What luck could bring them to him?
And then, through the fog,
Love suddenly appeared—
Clear in shape, distinct in scent,
Freeing his spirit to soar.
This love enveloped his broken grammar,
His flawed spelling,
Bringing peace to his heart and body.
Yet with love came chaos,
A sweet whirlwind of confusion.
And then, as the voice called,
"The next station is WAKE-UP,"

He opened his eyes.
And he rushed off the bus.

Mirage

The closer I approach your essence,
The farther you drift from your original form.
The more I magnify through the lens,
The more you disappear from your true image.

I behold the galaxy,
A world of wonder,
Dali, Munch, Picasso, Seurat...

In the end, you remain but a point,
A point that fades into nostalgia,
Nostalgia that melts into tears,
Tears that flow into an oasis.

I reach for your body within the lens,
But alas, I touch only a mirage.

Across the Date Line

Crossing the date line, soaring through the sky,
I wish this moment marked a shift in our bond.
As unbreakable as an eternal union,
As beautiful as a silk-woven knot,
As peaceful as a stream in a quiet valley at night.

The date changes,
So does life.
But you, you remain unchanged.

Between the Waves

I am a bird soaring over the ocean of heartbreak,
Ten days in flight, never resting,
Ten days that feel like lifetimes for a human soul.
I am a lonely bird, my wing shattered by an unseen stone.
The ocean stretches, vast and desolate,
No island of refuge in sight.
But then, through the storm, I glimpse a small speck,
A palm tree rising, a vision of fantasy at sea.

Yes, it is your nest,
Still, tender, safe, and inviting.
Do not tempt me with your whispered call,
To rest there, to stop for a while.

Let me pass without tears clouding my flight,
Let me keep singing, let me keep soaring,
Though my voice is hoarse, stained with blood,
Though my wings ache with every beat.

I fly on,

Until I discover an island of healing,
Where the breeze can mend my broken wing,
And one day, I can recover from this heartache.

Sipping on Solitude

Let's raise a toast to all the emotions of the coming year!
A champagne filled with despair, dark desires, loneliness, and failure,
With hopelessness, anguish, suffering, obsession, and selfishness,
With greed, extremity, jealousy, explosions, indifference, and ignorance,
And above all, to love, desperately addicted.
Cheers!

Erasing Your Name

This is the final verse I write,
Before the act of forgetting you.
Like all endings, it needs a symbolic ritual.
Leaves fall, resting in winter's lull,
Yet spring brings them back, reborn in hope.
But the stillness of the cold has come to an end in you.

I will forget you,
Like a station forgets its travelers
Once the train has left.
Like a butterfly forgets the scent of a flower
That once held her.

But before I forget you,
I write this last poem,
A small tribute to civility—political correctness
To erase the tattoo that is your name
Carved upon my heart.

Before I forget you,
I pronounce your name one last time,

As a dying bird sings its final song.
Adieu, Mr. Forgotten

Protocol for Your Return

When you return someday,
Let me first cut your nails,
Worn from the marks of your solitude.

When you return while I still breathe,
Let me comb through your hair,
Tangled by the weight of desperate nights.

When you return before this song fades,
Let me sing for you,
To cleanse your ears of sweet lies you've heard.

When you return while autumn wears its grace,
Let me dress in pure white,
To quiet the harsh colors of deceit you've encountered.

When you return while I stand in the shower,
Let me whistle, ignoring you for a while,
Let the tears of repentance fall outside,
For at least a "couple" of days,
for not having been a "couple" for so long.

May I Ask you A Favor?

Please,
No Christmas card this year.
Let silence linger, shrouded in mist,
Unburdened by the weight of karma's knot.

The cord that bound us has dissolved,
Let us drift now, like the distant moon,
Like the wind, the fog,
A dream forever out of reach,
An abstract painting,
An unsolved riddle.

So, my dear,
No card this year,
Nor any year to come.

Teardrops in the Crowd

Beneath the glow of splendid neon,
The festival hums with strangers' songs—
Laughter, applause, a dance-filled throng.
Yet, I retreat to shadows, alone, withdrawn.

A café corner, dim and still,
Gray table, black coffee, a bitter fill.
Eyes closed like a wilting bloom,
Your silhouette lingers, a fragrant gloom.

Tears fall softly, a hushed stream,
The music murmurs, "Don't dream, it's over."
Things feel surreal.
While joy outside feels worlds away, a rover.

I force a smile, let desolation unfold,
Among the crowd, a heart turns cold.
Until I find, in this quiet grace,
A crowd encircled in my lonely space.

Fade Out

Forgive my cunning, my fragile guise,
For I tread your swamp of love's thin lies.
Wandering lost in circles deep,
Through dusky words where secrets creep.

Shaky truths in risky schemes,
Whisky-laden, shadowed dreams.
Hypocrite hearts in innocence veiled,
A masquerade where none prevailed.

But as this mournful tune expires,
Our weary withered romance dims its fires.
Fading now, cheap sentiments fall,
A quiet end to it all.

A Heart in Grayscale

Autumn blooms wither and fade,
Leaves weep softly, one by one laid.
They carry the scent of sorrow's hush,
The wind, damp with grief, whispering dread.
Darkness swirls in solitude's grasp,
A quiet twinge in its tender clasp.

Alone I stand in this empty field,
Desiring breath that wounds could heal.
Under the sunset's solitary flow,
I see your soul's glow.

The autumn sky wears gray each night,
Birds silence their songs, forsaking flight.
Butterflies cease their delicate waltz,
Even the bee's sting feels no faults.

Since you've gone, the world's colors fade,
All is gray, all black—life's hue decayed.
Hollow and still, a shadowed span,
Yearning for light, where life began.
Return to me with hope's bright flame,

Infuse my world with your magic, with your name.

Winy Silence Along the Vines

Silence weeps beneath the vineyard,
Rooted deep in the shadow of oak trees.
It transforms into a wine-tinted rhapsody,
A melody steeped in sorrow's tone.
Silence waits for the bloom of spring,
For splendor's tender, golden wing.

It lingers on the stems of dewy orchids,
Carries nostalgia through endless ages.
As summer nights yearn for autumn's glow,
Silence sobs for a moonlit sorrow.
It touches all life with a cruel gesture,
Whispering truths from hearts displaced.

Silence sharpens the fragile air.
Unspoken lies pierce its brittle heights.
Filling the land with gloomy blooms.

Farewell, in the Gale

On a sunlit day, you soared with the haze,
It was the final warmth that reached my gaze.

On a rainy evening, you vanished in the storm,
The last drops of rain whispered your form.

On a tempest's day, you were swept by the gale,
It was the final shiver, lost in the wail.

A Masochist's Love Song

Let more blood spill from my shattered heart,
Let this wound grow deeper, sharper still,
Let my loneliness twist tighter with pain,
Let my soul thirst like a desert's dry breath,
Let this scratch burn fiercer,
Let me fall to the ground and never rise again,
Let all this suffering be born of you.

Let my rebirth lie in your heartbeat,
This anguish of poetry carving through my skin,
Let my bones crumble to dust,
Enduring this ache that shapes my soul,
Let this wound become the molten core of a forgotten crater.

Let this affliction remain eternal,
Even in the void of nothingness.

III
Nature and Gaze

Heartbeat of Poetry

Poetry exists to refresh the soul,
To reignite the spark of energy,
To hydrate life,
To offer release from karma,
To break free from rigid thoughts,
To clear away the haze,
To convey desire,
To capture fleeting moments,
To embellish the world,
To weave silence into melody,
To transcend the boundaries of time,
To echo the universe within.

Poetry, to elevate the spirit,
To take a surreal promenade.

The Language of Omega

From my mother's womb,
A language born to soothe my soul in sorrow,
The language of my essence,
The language that fills my dreams.
It leads me to Nirvana,
Where my heart strolls in peaceful tranquility.
The language of the Land of Morning Calm.

Oh, my mother tongue!
In your bosom, I find my home,
I kiss you, lost in love.

Questions of Alchemy of Six Elements

I turn the noise into stillness.
I carry the secrets of humankind within me.
I understand the sorrow of a woman's tears in the rain.
Who am I but the rock?

I converse with lonely souls in the velvet of the night.
I ignite inspiration for poets in despair.
I evoke the most surreal desires.
Who am I but the moon?

I touch the sphere of forgotten memories.
I breathe out noble emotions.
I gently touch the leaves of the changing seasons.
Who am I but the wind?

I feel the whisper of the sea breeze.
I seek truth in the heart of nature.
I sing in the tranquil pace of time.
Who am I but the river?

I spread the branches of wisdom.
I transform light into life-giving air.
I plant the seeds of love in the very heart of the sky.
Who am I but the tree?

I forgive the whims of the sky, the rain, and the snow.
I embrace the ever-renewing splendor of nature.
I am reborn each day with hope.
Who am I but the earth?

Black Pearl

The nocturnal sighs of ages dwell within your being,
Dark as the void of a distant black hole,
Round as the endless circle of time.
You are the eye of immutable truth,
You are the molten core of years of sorrow.

You are the eruption of ecstasy,
Your body, a sphere of infinite night,
Your soul, the dreamlike glow of moonlight.

Jade

You echo the solitude of a star that has fallen
beside a quiet oriental garden.
You inhale the life force of every shade of green
from herbs to grasses, from leaves to trees,
spanning the entire universe.

You are the weeping of a princess
from a land of verdant gold.
You are frozen in a sphere both regal and untamed.

Within your being, within your spirit,
Eternity finds its rest.
Serenity breathes its inspiration.

Sunflower's Identity

Reaching for the sun in the name of freedom,
Proclaiming truth with a fervent cry,
Praying for the fruit of joy to ripen,
Harmonizing to the rhythm of peace,
Yearning for unity of life's mysterious forms.

Each petal aspires a sanctuary of light,
You are the sacred root of a fearless heart, boldly radiant,
You are the echo of a forgotten Luminous Dynasty.

Here, only the craving in your breath is felt,
Only the depths of your silent desire are heard.

You stretch toward the sun's nostalgic warmth,
You awaken the moon's enchanted essence.
From your timeless bloom,
A seed of passion takes hold,
A gesture of desire unfolds,
All from the core of your sunlit instinct.

An Interview with a Poet

Q: What drives you to write poetry?
A: Because poetry invites me for coffee,
Because poetry asks to share a meal,
Because poetry pleads for love,
Because poetry promises eternal devotion,
Because poetry says it needs solitude for a while,
Because poetry tells me lies, sweet lies,
Because poetry is difficult to control,
Because poetry is stubborn,
Because poetry seeks a moment of joy,
Because poetry tempts me endlessly,
Because poetry waits for me, ever patient,
Because poetry gazes at me, unmasked,
Because poetry craves a touch of trickery and magic.

Hydrotherapy

Water is a sensual dream,
Voluptuous lips that whisper,
A tender caress,
A guiding current,
A lover's pull—
Yet never my release.
Water carries the taste of wine,
The gaze of a voyeur,
The wandering heart of a stroller.
It heals me, it frees me,
Yet binds me still.

Discrete and indiscrete,
Like you,
Water hides her secrets,
Holds her body and soul apart,
Yet entwines them in love's fever.
Water desires.
And loves desire.
I dive into her depths—
The past and future merge.
And in that plunge,
I am absent from the present.

Ode to Vanity

Vanity fondles me,
Feeds me, sustains me,
Walks beside me,
A shadow entwined with my being.

Vanity shapes my vision,
Colors my world anew,
Becomes my compass,
My spirit's guide,
The fountainhead of my poetic soul.

Vanity, vanity, my dearest muse!
Together, we waltz —
Through the night's silken shadow,
Through life's final breath,
Forever my intimate friend, my soulmate.

A Story Behind the Altar of Poetry

Before the collective poetry book saw the light,
Mr. Austere Priest, the coordinator,
Demanded that my "Nirvana" bow to "Heaven."
All day, he preached, advised,
And pressed upon me his holy verdict.

I stood firm, defending my word,
A whisper of Buddhist serenity.
But his persistence thundered louder,
A relentless storm of Christian creed.
In his eyes, my defiance was sin,
And I felt the flames of his damnation.

The coordinator—oh, devil in disguise—
Had the final word,
And "Heaven" replaced my sacred "Nirvana."
The book was born,
Yet my heart resides in Nirvana still.
Alas, I am the unsung martyr of poetry.

A Prehistoric Song from the Cave

* Written in the cave of Anakai Tangata, Easter Island (Rapa Nui), Chile

Here, within my mother's womb,
I ready myself for the journey outward.
The ocean beckons, its vastness calling.

This cave, my sanctuary,
The center where I am nourished,
A cradle of my prenatal being,
My prehistory unfolding.

Here, calm and chaos intertwine,
In the navel of the universe,
I exist.
I do not exist yet.
I once existed.

Before I sail into infinity,
I breathe, I give,
Oxygen flows through the umbilical cord
That stretches toward the cosmos.

The Hermit's Thesis

It is the deep breath of a hermit,
Dwelling in a secluded temple.
A lone surfer battling the night's storm.
It is the sharp eye of a jeweler,
The quiet knowing of a potter's perfection.
It is the escaped cry of "Eureka" from Archimedes,
A moment of discovery in the silence of thought.

It is living with the moods of all seasons,
In a single, ever-changing day:
Spring's euphoria,
Summer's passion,
Autumn's melancholy,
Winter's reflection.

Writing a thesis is grasping the cosmic web—
Indra's net,
Where all is interwoven,
Each strand, a part of the whole.

Into the Spring Light

I've eaten two leaves of aromatic clover,
To sate the hunger of my soul,
Longing to devour your splendor,
Beneath the sun that dances like a crystal breeze.

Caress me, submerge me in your lake,
Relive my hurt, my unquenched thirst.

Here I wait, thirsting for another leaf of clover,
For in your gift, my hunger fades,
And fullness leads me to tranquility.

Your sensual tenderness draws near,
Oh, dear Springtime, save my body, save my soul.

Library Philosopher

Each day, I see four digits, no, eight,
Always linked by a hyphen,
The first four and the last four.
One is born; one fades away.
We record these digits with cold indifference,
But alas, they vanish.
Only etched in printed words.
Ah, will I too one day be inked in such print?
Some disappear, others return,
Souls marked by eight digits, others without markings.
What separates these two paths?
Will they ever meet?
One day, when life begins with five digits,
But will Christ have come by then?
And death ends with five or six,
How will the world be altered? Where will I be?
What future does the meaning of life aspire to?
From here, to where?
From now, to which dimension of time?
Lives and souls, tangled in the shelves of books,
Page after page, filled with passions and struggles.
But where have all the geniuses gone?

The Tapestry of Sunshine and Shade

Shade, once lonely and lost,
Yearned for the breath of life from Sunshine's warmth.
She longed to feel the light that would bring her peace,
Her fate, a silent wait in the depths of despair.

Then, one day, Sun rose, casting her glow,
Filling Shadow's being with a rush of emotion.
But soon, the light faded, and Sun was gone,
Leaving Shade in tears, her fear of loneliness reborn.
She retreated into the cave of winter's chill,
Seeking solace in the quiet, the cold.

Yet, Sun returned once more, transformed,
A hue of wisdom, serenity in its touch.
No longer did Shade feel the sting of solitude,
For she understood that separation was fleeting,
That she and Sunshine were two parts of the same whole.

And so, Shade and Sunshine, side by side,
Thrived in harmony, in cosmic energy,
Where the solar and lunar essences forever sustain them.

Invisible Yet Visible

Some believe you dwell in Heaven,
Others say you live within us.
Some claim you're spread across the vast Universe,
While others find you in the rhythm of Nature.
Some say you can only be seen in the mind's eye,
And Nietzsche declares that you are dead.

O Almighty Sacred,
What is this breath that touches my soul?
What is this whisper, bright with Aurora's glow?

On a dark summer night, I alone called your name.
From a garden where only silence reigned.
A sudden breeze stirred the branches,
And they began to dance, creating a haven of joy.

I saw the word LOVE floating all around,
Wrapping my body and soul in its embrace.
The air smelled of fruits and flowers in harvest,

Radiating with the rainbow's colors, dazzling and bright.
I saw a spectrum of in-between shades uniting seven rays,
And in that moment, I felt a seed fall into my being.
My soul was purified, my body adorned,

O Sacred Almighty,
This is the tale of my son's conception,
Witnessed only by the night's breeze,
And the aura of your mystery.

From the Golden Hill

From the realms of myth,
the Goddess of Peace appears,
Gracefully, she descends, bright and divine.

All are stunned by her mystical grace,
Mesmerized by the splendor in her gaze,
Entranced by the sparkle of her movements,
Whole in the magic of her golden touch.

Before us, our Utopian dreams unfold,
Expanding, radiant, gleaming with light,
Laid out upon the Golden Hill of Peace.

Together, we sing, "Dreams come true. Keep the faith!"
She stands at the heart of the altar,
Delivering a message of peace to the world,
Radiating the purest joy in a crystalline form,
Filling the air with an eternal fragrance of mystery.

Zafira, the Minimalist

* Zafira is my minimalist cat born in July 2014.

A gentle touch, a sip of water,
A simple meal to keep her body afloat.
A basket lined with grains of sand,
Enough for all her little needs.
A wisp of breeze, a patch of grass,
The whisper of flowers in the air,
A gentle word spoken, a satiny zephyr,
A collar bearing her name — not jewels,
No diamonds, no sapphires to bear.
A warm blanket to ward off the chill,
A small vial to guard her health,
The sun's golden kiss, the moon's soft glow,
And tender strokes from a loving hand.
In these small treasures, joy abides—
Enough for her, perhaps for all.
Let Zafira teach us what we need:
The art of living with so little.

To My Supreme Sphere

You lull the tremors of my heartaches,
Guarding the silent rivers of my tears.
You've watched over my nights of solitude,
Shared in my screams, my scars, my refusals—
And in my joy, my desire, my fleeting bliss.

Your texture weaves through my verses,
Your scent ignites the flames within me.
Your form, a fragile truce
Between my melancholy and my ecstasy.

At your core lies my unspoken truth
On your edges, the ghost of my faltering touch.
One end of your diameter reveals sunrise,
The other, a sunset imbued with sensitivity.
Each marked by desires I dare not name.

Oh, my Supreme Sphere,
Wrap my soul in the tender grace of your sensual arms.

Meditation on Peeing

Have the remnants of desire
finally drained away?
Or does a fresh, untainted yearning
quietly rise in its place?
The hidden traces of long-held worry,
Wrapped in golden ribbons, flow down,
Forming a single verse.

Gather your greed, anger, and folly.
Cast them off without regret.
Let relinquish stories unworthy of memoirs,
Of passions extinguished halfway.

Allow the pee and the poem
To come forth naturally,
Raw and unfiltered.

Let them surge.
Offer them to the waiting void.
Pour your desire, unreserved,
Into the golden rays of a poem.

Dandelion's Blaze

No radiant rhetoric,
No instant charm,
Yet with calm resolve alone,
For days, for years,
It pierced through every crack it found.

With one fierce passion,
It blazed in brilliant yellow,
Its body worn by the fiery path,
Splintered in quiet endurance,
Fractured, yet steadfast.
At times it faltered, bending low,
Yet with unyielding will, it rose again,
Reaching slowly, steadily upward,
Transforming green against the sky.

Those who have tasted solitude,
Those who have grasped the weight of determination,
Those who have sensed the fragrance of such despair,
Would never pass this bloom unseen.

Too painfully beautiful,
Bursting through the wall's cold cracks,
The unconquered spirit of a dandelion.

Along the Veins of Nature

Like the quiet moon,
Rising from behind autumn clouds,
You enter the solitary sphere of my soul,
Season's allure in calm repose,
Inverted reeds in a mist-kissed field.

All that can be seen are your moist eyes,
Glimmering beneath the playful moonlight.
What is this moment shared, between you and I?
The waves of wildness sweep in,
Carrying epics of endlessness...

Midnight's pulse softens,
Melting with the sweetness of your breath.

Love me always.
Oh, my Nature,
Let your lips veil my thirsty ones,
Awaken my dormant truth with your touch of magic.

A Butterfly in Blue

A fire burns within my soul,
One glance, and a bell begins to toll,
Another look, and all is lost,
A fleeting moment, a world, a cost.

A lonely butterfly in blue,
Yearning to reach the sky so true,
From her wings, freedom's seed takes flight,
Spreading toward the cosmic light.

As she sings, the universe holds its breath,
Spellbound by her voice, hope flourishes
A whirl of enchantment, senses awake,
All open to love, for love's sweet sake.

She caresses the stars with graceful hands,
They shape a constellation of metamorphosis,
Once timid, hidden from view,
Now her eyes shine, brave and true.

In her heart so deep,
She sowed love in soil so steep.

A butterfly in blue,
Still dancing in love, still singing true,
Falling forever in love, in blue.

The Captain's Song

Before the year slips away,
I must read and close the pending books
Left adrift on the waves.
The harp's melodies, long paused,
Must now resume,
And truly repose within me.
I'll send the letters I never dared,
I'll decode the Morse I delayed to decrypt.
I'll retrieve the verses
Lost in the storm inside,
And cast them beyond the bow,
To bask in the green sunlight.
Leaving behind the gods of solitude,
I'll journey first to that island.
I'll search for the lost compass,
And find the lighthouse that calls without end.
I'll trace a current of dreams
Swaying in the endless sea,
Seeking you, seeking me,
Finding the you within me,
And the me within you,
Where the sky merges with the ocean.
That eternal, tranquil realm of Dharma.

Epilogue

Junghwa Splendor Kim
from Santiago, Chile, May 2025

Pondering Stars on the Pond is a carefully gathered constellation of my poems; an illumination of a journey that spans three decades. These verses, as the title suggests, will invite you to pause, to gaze inward, and to discover calm ripples in the depths of your soul. For me, poetry crossed the borders of language, weaving Korean, English, Spanish, and French into a mosaic of imagination and feeling, until finally converging into the birth of this collection of poems in English.

I aim to be a writer who ignites joy and happiness to readers by presenting poetry as a form of healing for those going through moments of despair. I hope my verses inspire people to view everyday objects and phenomena through a new perspective, discovering deeper insights along the way. My voice has been melodically shaped by the French Symbolists—Mallarmé, Rimbaud, Verlaine, and Valéry—whose synesthetic orchestration of words cast a spell on me. Inspired by their picturesque perfume, I sought to embroider hues of emotion and sensation into my verses.

To be a poet is to dream—to unearth miracles in the mundane, to glimpse utopias hidden within the stream of the everyday. The desire to find poetic truth led me on a magical journey to Chile, a land that has produced two Nobel laureates in poetry—Pablo Neruda and Gabriela Mistral. For a time, I wandered, yearning to hear echoes of their voices in every corner. But poetry, I learned, is not bound to any place or "topia." It takes root in the heart, blooming in eyes unshackled by convention, brimming with purity and freedom.

If even a single line from this collection lingers in your heart — etched in memory, written on paper, or reshaping the way you see the world — then this journey may have been fulfilled. Making this book see the light feels like finally fulfilling the long-held debts of my soul, a liberation both significant and long overdue. With gratitude for the boundless dream of poetry, to all starry souls who ponder upon the poetic pond, I lift a toast to you: *¡Salud!*

Acknowledgements

To the aches that have etched the fabric of time;
To the pauses that captured my breaths;
To the melodies that blossom within the voids;
To the lunar glow infusing my lonely pen;
To the streams imparting the virtue of patience in their turn and return;
To the tears that sculpted me into resilience, and at times, fragility;
To the invisible forces of the universe, orchestrating my words before I discovered them;
To the transient instances—those subtle co-conspirators;
To the voices that spoke not in words, but in presence, steady as the tide.
To a kindred soul—a serene guiding light on this path;
To the cosmic harmonies embracing despair and joy—gracing these pages;
And to the *Pondering Stars on the Pond*—ready to shine for you.

www.ingramcontent.com/pod-product-compliance
Lightning Source LLC
LaVergne TN
LVHW041339080426
835512LV00006B/529